CURRIES & SIMMERING POT

Contents

D0450190

Cooking pots tend to impart their own flavors to the food cooked in them and the handi, kadhai and tawa contribute in no small measure to the distinctiveness of Indian cuisine. The dumpukht or sealed pot style of cooking, in which the pot is sealed with a layer of dough and a partially cooked dish is placed on smouldering coals so that the food, simmering slowly for hours, matures in its own juices and steam, preserves all the flavors and aromas of the ingredients used intact. Though it originated in Persia, dumpukht has been perfected to a fine art in India, giving each dish a character of its own. The recipes given in this section, however, have all been adapted for cooking in the oven and on the open gas flame. Dishes that require constant stirring and scraping of masala are generally cooked in the handi or kadhai. However, a heavy-bottomed saucepan can also be used.

CHICKEN HANDI LAZEEZ

Literally, delectable chicken from the cooking pot.

Ingredients

Boneless chicken thighs	2 lb	Ginger paste	¾ oz/4 tsp
Cardamoms	4	Onions, sliced	2½ oz/⅓ cup
Chicken stock	16 fl oz/2 cups	Refined oil	2½ fl oz/5 tbs
Cinnamon	1" stick	Saffron	a pinch
Cloves	10	Salt to taste	
Garlic paste	¾ oz/4 tsp	Red chilli powder	⅛ oz/½ tsp
Garlic, chopped	1 oz/2 tbs		

Method

1. Cut chicken into bite-sized pieces. Soak saffron in a little water in a spoon for 10 minutes. Crush and keep aside.

2. Heat oil in a saucepan and add chopped garlic. Sauté till brown. Add the onions and sauté till light brown. Add cinnamon, cloves and cardamoms and sauté till the onions turn golden brown.

3. Add the ginger and garlic pastes, chicken, salt and red chilli powder. Stir for 3-4 minutes. Add chicken stock and bring to boil. Cover and simmer till chicken is tender.

4. Remove from fire. Take out the chicken pieces from the gravy. Strain the gravy into another pot through a soup strainer.

5. Cook the gravy till reduced to a sauce-like consistency. Add the chicken pieces and cook for a minute.

Tips

Time
Preparation: 20 minutes
Cooking: 30 minutes

To Serve
Stir in the prepared saffron and serve hot with an Indian bread of your choice

KHATTE CHICKEN

A rich, tart chicken dish, served with embellishments and many accompaniments.

Ingredients

Chicken breasts	12	Green chillies, chopped	4
Almond paste	1½ oz/3 tbs	Lemon juice	1 fl oz/2 tbs
Black pepper powder	¼ oz/1 tsp	Onions, cut in rings	5 oz/⅔ cup
Cumin (*jeera*) seeds	¼ oz/1 tsp	Saffron	a pinch, dissolved in 1 tbs milk
Capsicum, cut in rings	3 oz	Salt to taste	
Garlic paste	¾ oz/4 tsp	White butter	2 oz/4 tbs
Ginger paste	¾ oz/4 tsp	Yoghurt	8¾ oz/1 cup

Method

1. Hang yoghurt in a cheese cloth until reduced by half. Meanwhile, clean and debone chicken breasts.

2. Make a marinade of yoghurt, ginger and garlic pastes, salt, cumin, black pepper, lemon, green chillies and almond paste and marinate the chicken in it for half an hour.

3. Grease an oven proof shallow dish. Place the chicken pieces in it, without overlapping.

Arrange the onion and capsicum rings over the chicken pieces and pour the left over marinade evenly over it.

4. Dot with dollops of remaining butter and roast in a preheated oven at 300 °F for 20 minutes.

5. Remove, sprinkle saffron, cover and let simmer in the oven for another 10 minutes.

Time
Preparation: 45 minutes
Cooking: 20 minutes

To Serve
Uncover dish, wipe edges and serve simmering hot with roti, raita and chutney recipes for which are given in the other two sections of this book

PEPPER KOZI CHETTINAD

The famous black peppercorns of South India make this chicken delicacy a hot favorite and give it a special flavor.

Ingredients

Chicken	2½ lb	Groundnut/peanut oil	2 fl oz/4 tbs
Black peppercorns	¾ oz/4 tsp	Lemon juice	1 fl oz/2 tbs
Coriander leaves, chopped	1 oz/6 tsp	Onions, chopped	6 oz/¾ cup
Garam masala	¼ oz/1 tsp	Salt to taste	
Garlic paste	1½ oz/3 tbs	Tomatoes, chopped	5 oz/⅔ cup
Ginger paste	1½ oz/3 tbs	Yoghurt	4 oz/½ cup

Method

1. Clean and cut the chicken into 8 pieces each.

2. Pound the peppercorns with a pestle. whip the yoghurt and add the peppercorns, half the ginger and garlic pastes, lemon juice and salt. Mix well and marinate the chicken pieces in it for at least 30 minutes.

3. Meanwhile, heat oil in a handi. Add onions and sauté over medium heat until light brown. Add the remaining ginger and garlic pastes and sauté until onions are golden brown. Add the tomatoes and stir-cook till the fat appears on the sides of the pan.

4. Add the chicken along with the marinade and stir for 4-5 minutes. Add 8 fl oz/1 cup water and bring to boil.

5. Cover and let simmer, stirring occasionally until the chicken is tender. Adjust the seasoning. Sprinkle garam masala and stir.

Tips

Time
Preparation: 1 hour
Cooking: 30 minutes

To Serve
Garnish with coriander leaves and serve with boiled rice or roti

METHI CHICKEN

Chicken cooked with either dry fenugreek leaves or fresh fenugreek is a connoisseur's delight. For best results use fresh leaves.

Ingredients

Chicken	2.2 lb/2 small birds, cut into 6 pieces each	Garlic, chopped	1 oz/2 tbs
		Ginger, slivers	1 oz/2 tbs
Cardamoms	5	Ginger juliennes	¾ oz/4 tsp
Cinnamon	1" stick	Green chillies, slit	5
Cloves	8	Oil	2½ fl oz/⅓ cup
Coriander leaves, chopped	½ oz/1 tbs	Onions, chopped	12 oz/1½ cups
Dough to seal casserole		Red chilli powder	¼ oz/1 tsp
Fenugreek (*methi*),		Salt to taste	
dry leaves	½ oz/1 tbs	Tomatoes, chopped	8¾ oz/1 cup
or fresh leaves	2 oz/¼ cup	Yoghurt	8¾ oz/1 cup

Method

1. Marinate chicken in whipped yoghurt and salt for half an hour.

2. Meanwhile, heat fat in a kadhai, crackle cardamoms, cloves and cinnamon. Add onions and sauté till golden brown. Stir in chopped garlic, ginger and green chillies. Add red chilli powder and tomatoes and stir-cook till fat surfaces.

3. Add chicken with the marinade and 8 fl oz/1 cup water. Bring to boil, cover and simmer till the fat is visible on the sides once again and the chicken is tender.

4. Remove to an oven proof casserole, sprinkle with fenugreek, ginger juliennes and coriander, cover and seal with dough. Place in a preheated oven at 325 °F for 15 minutes.

Tips

Time
Preparation: 45 minutes
Cooking: 45 minutes

To Serve
Open casserole and serve simmering hot with any Indian bread

KADHAI CHICKEN

A tomato based chicken delicacy cooked in the Indian wok and flavored strongly with fenugreek and coriander.

Ingredients

Chicken	2.2 lb/2 birds, cut into 8 pieces each	Green chillies, slit	4
Coriander leaves	1 oz/2 tbs	Dry fenugreek leaves	¼ oz/1 tsp
Coriander seeds, pounded	¼ oz/1 tsp	Oil	2½ fl oz/⅓ cup
Garam masala	¼ oz/1 tsp	Red chillies, whole, pounded	8
Garlic paste	¾ oz/4 tsp	Salt to taste	
Ginger, chopped	1½ oz/3 tbs	Tomatoes, chopped	2.2 lb

Method

1. Heat oil in a wok. Sauté garlic paste till brown. Add the pounded red chillies and the freshly pounded coriander seeds and stir for a few seconds. Add the tomatoes and bring to a boil. Add half the coriander leaves and all the ginger, slit green chillies and salt. Simmer for 5 minutes.

2. Add the chicken and simmer, stirring occasionally till the gravy thickens and the chicken is tender.

3. Once the fat surfaces, stir in the garam masala and the dry fenugreek leaves. Cook for 2 minutes.

Tips

Time
Preparation: 40 minutes
Cooking: 30 minutes

To Serve
Garnish with coriander and serve with naan or roti

KOZI VARTA CURRY

Boneless chicken pieces simmered in a spicy gravy.

Ingredients

Chicken	2½ lb	Ginger paste	1½ oz/3 tbs
Black peppercorns, pounded	⅛ oz/½ tsp	Groundnut/peanut oil	2½ fl oz/⅓ cup
Cardamom powder	⅛ oz/½ tsp	Lemon juice	½ fl oz/3 tsp
Clove powder	a pinch	Onions, chopped	2½ oz/⅓ cup
Cinnamon powder	a pinch	Red chilli powder	⅛ oz/½ tsp
Coriander leaves, chopped	¾ oz/4 tsp	Salt to taste	
Coriander powder	⅛ oz/½ tsp	Tamarind (*imlee*)	1 oz/6 tsp
Curry leaves	12	Tomatoes, chopped	4 oz/½ cup
Garlic paste	1 oz/6 tsp	Turmeric (*haldi*) powder	¼ oz/1 tsp

Method

1. Clean the chicken, debone and cut into 1½ inch cubes.
2. Mix red chillies, turmeric and salt with half of the ginger and garlic pastes and rub this marinade onto the chicken pieces. Keep aside for 30 minutes.
3. Heat oil in a wok, add the marinated chicken and sauté over medium heat until evenly light brown.
4. Remove the chicken and reserve the oil.
5. Soak the tamarind in ¾ fl oz/4 teaspoons water. After 10 minutes, mash well, squeeze out the pulp and discard. Keep extract aside.
6. Reheat the reserved oil, add the curry leaves and stir over medium heat for 30 seconds. Add onions and sauté until light brown. Add the remaining ginger and garlic pastes, stir for a minute, add the tomatoes and stir. Cook till the fat appears on the sides of the pan. Add the cardamom, coriander, clove and cinnamon powders, and stir for a minute. Add the tamarind and cook for 5 minutes.
7. Add the chicken pieces and simmer for 8-10 minutes. Add 8 fl oz/1 cup water and bring to boil. Reduce to medium heat and cook, stirring constantly until the moisture has evaporated and the masala coats the chicken pieces.
8. Sprinkle with pepper and lemon juice.

Tips

Time
Preparation: 1 hour
Cooking: 45 minutes

To Serve
Remove to a flat dish, garnish with green coriander and serve with dosa (for recipe see p. 8 of the **Vegetarian Dishes & Desserts** section) and paratha (for recipe see p. 61 of the **Tandoor & Dry Dishes** section)

MAKHANI CHICKEN

This rich, roast chicken delicacy is a favorite with most North Indians.

Ingredients

Tandoori chicken	2.2 lb/2 birds, cut into 8 pieces each	Ginger paste	1½ oz/3 tbs
		Ginger, shredded	¼ oz/1 tsp
Butter	4 oz/½ cup	Green chillies	5
Coriander leaves, chopped	½ oz/1 tbs	Paprika	⅛ oz/½ tsp
Cream	5 fl oz/⅔ cup	Salt to taste	
Garlic paste	1½ oz/3 tbs	Tomatoes, chopped	2 lb

Method

1. Melt half the butter in a pot, stir in the ginger and garlic pastes and cook till the mixture is dry.

2. Add tomatoes and salt and cook till the tomatoes are mashed. Add 16 fl oz/2 cups water and simmer for a few minutes.

3. Strain the gravy through a soup strainer into another pot.

4. Melt the remaining butter in a wok, add the shredded ginger and green chillies and sauté for a minute. Add the paprika and wait for the color of the masala to turn a bright red.

5. Add the strained gravy and bring to a boil. Add the tandoori chicken pieces and simmer for 10 minutes till the chicken is tender. Stir in the cream.

Tips

Time

Preparation: 20 minutes plus time to roast the chicken if tandoori chicken is not available. For recipe of tandoori chicken see p. 3 of the ***Tandoor & Dry Dishes*** section

Cooking: 45 minutes

To Serve

Garnish with coriander leaves and serve with any Indian bread of your choice

RAAN-E-MURGH

This delicacy is considered to be one of the best chicken dishes. The marinated chicken is roasted in an oven before it is immersed in a smooth gravy.

Ingredients

Chicken drumsticks	2 lb	Lemon juice	1 fl oz/2 tbs
Cashew nuts, crushed		Onion paste, browned	3 oz/6 tbs
and browned	½ oz/1 tbs	Red chilli powder	¼ oz/1 tsp
Chicken stock	32 fl oz/4 cups	Saffron	a pinch
Coriander powder	¼ oz/1 tsp	Salt to taste	
Cream	1 fl oz/2 tbs	Sweet ittar	2 drops
Garlic paste	1 oz/2 tbs	Tomato purée	32 fl oz/4 cups
Ginger paste	1 oz/2 tbs	White butter	3 oz/6 tbs
Green chillies, sliced	2		

Method

1. Marinate the chicken in the ginger and garlic pastes, salt, chilli powder and lemon juice for an hour.

2. Skewer the chicken pieces and cook in the tandoor till half done.

3. In a large pan cook the onion paste, tomato purée and chicken stock till it reaches a sauce like consistency. Strain through a cheese/or straner cloth or strainer.

4. In a wok heat 2 oz/4 tbs butter. Add coriander powder and chicken pieces and sauté for 3-4 minutes. Add the sauce and cook for another 3 to 4 minutes.

5. Add sweet ittar and remove to a bowl.

6. Melt the remaining butter in a small pan. Add the green chillies and sauté briefly. Add the cashew nuts and cream and pour onto the dish. Crush saffron in a spoon with a few drops of water and sprinkle over the cashew-cream paste.

Tips

Time
Preparation: 30 minutes
Cooking: 45 minutes

To Serve
Serve hot with an Indian bread of your choice

KHUROOS-E-TURSH

Chicken breasts stuffed with a spicy, onion-capsicum mixture and baked individually in foil.

Ingredients

Chicken breasts	8
Almonds	1¼ oz/20-24
Black cumin	
(*shah jeera*) seeds	¼ oz/1 tsp
Capsicum, shredded	2 oz/¼ cup
Garlic	1¼ oz/15 cloves
Ginger	1¼ oz/3" piece
Green chillies, chopped fine	10
Lemon juice	4 fl oz/½ cup
Mint leaves	¼ oz/1 tsp
Oil for basting	
Onion, shredded	14 oz/1⅔ cups
Processed cheese, grated	4 oz/½ cup
Saffron	a large pinch soaked in 1 tsp water
Salt and pepper to taste	
Yoghurt, hung	6 oz/¾ cup

Method

1. Clean chicken. In a blender, make a paste of ginger, garlic and mint, using as little water as possible.
2. Mix together onion, capsicum, green chillies, yoghurt, grated cheese, lemon juice, salt, pepper, black cumin, saffron and almonds and add to the ginger-garlic paste.
3. Fill this stuffing into the chicken breasts.
4. Wrap each breast in aluminium foil and bake in a preheated oven at 325 °F for 15 minutes. Baste with oil and bake again for 5-7 minutes.

Tips

Time
Preparation: 45 minutes
Cooking: 20 minutes

To serve
Remove foil and serve hot with sheer-mal or naan. For recipes see pp. 62 and 64 of the **Tandoor & Dry Dishes** section

GOAN FISH CURRY

This spicy hot curry goes by the name of just Goa curry.
It is a traditional fish curry and is a regular at most Goan meals.

Ingredients

Sole on plaice	1¼ lb	Groundnut/peanut oil	2 fl oz/¼ cup
Coconut, grated	5 oz/⅔ cup	Lemon juice	2 fl oz/¼ cup
Coconut milk	5 fl oz/⅔ cup	Onions, chopped	2 oz/¼ cup
Coriander seeds	½ oz/1 tbs	Red chillies, whole	15
Cumin (*jeera*) seeds	¼ oz/1 tsp	Salt to taste	
Garlic paste	¼ oz/1 tsp	Tamarind (*imlee*), deseeded	1½ oz/3 tbs
Ginger paste	¾ oz/4 tsp	Tomatoes, chopped	2 oz/¼ cup
Green chillies	4	Turmeric (*haldi*) powder	¼ oz/1 tsp

Method

1. Sprinkle salt and lemon on the fish and marinade for an hour.
2. Meanwhile, blend the coconut, whole chillies, cumin seeds, coriander seeds, turmeric, tamarind and the ginger and garlic pastes together in a blender with the coconut milk.
3. Heat oil in a kadhai. Add the onions and sauté till golden brown. Add the tomatoes and cook for 3 to 4 minutes till the tomatoes are mashed.
4. Add the blended mixture and 8 fl oz/ 1 cup water and bring to boil. Add the green chillies and the fish and simmer for 7 minutes. Bring to a boil and then let simmer again for 2 minutes. Do not cover the pot at any stage while the curry is being cooked.

Tips

Time
Preparation: 45 minutes
Cooking: 30 minutes

To Serve
Remove to a bowl and serve with boiled rice

MACHHI KEBAB SAILANA

A tempting fried fish snack.

Ingredients

Fish	1 lb	Green chillies, chopped	1 oz/6 tsp
Breadcrumbs to coat		Oil to fry fish	
Coriander leaves, chopped	½ oz/3 tsp	Onions, chopped	6 oz/¾ cup
Eggs	2	Salt to taste	
Ginger, chopped	1 oz/6 tsp	Vinegar	1 fl oz/2 tbs

Method

1. Skin fish and remove bones. Cut into 3 inch × 2 inch cubes. Wash and pat dry on towel.

2. Soak chopped onions in the vinegar for an hour, then add ginger, green chillies, coriander leaves and salt and mix thoroughly.

3. Mix onion mixture with the fish pieces. Beat eggs in a separate pan. Dip fish pieces into the beaten eggs and then roll over breadcrumbs.

4. Press lightly to make coating firm and even. Shake off surplus crumbs.

5. Set aside for half an hour to let egg coating dry.

6. Heat oil in a pan and fry on moderate heat, a few kebabs at a time, till golden brown.

Time
Preparation: 1½ hours
Cooking: 30 minutes

To Serve
Drain fish on paper napkins and serve with lemon wedges

JHINGA DUM ANARI

Baked prawns with pomegranate.

Ingredients

Jumbo prawns	2 lb/8	Peas, fresh	4 oz/½ cup
Cheddar cheese	1 oz/2 tbs	Pickled onions,	
Coriander leaves chopped	¼ oz/1 tsp	chopped	2 oz/¼ cup
Cumin (*jeera*) seeds	⅛ oz/½ tsp	Pomegranate seeds	
Garlic paste	¼ oz/1 tsp	(*anaar dana*), fresh	8¾ oz/1 cup
Ginger, chopped fine	¼ oz/1 tsp	Salt to taste	
Ginger paste	¼ oz/1 tsp	Tomato ketchup	1½ fl oz/3 tbs
Lemon juice	1 fl oz/2 tbs	White pepper powder	⅛ oz/½ tsp
Malt vinegar	1 fl oz/2 tbs	Red chilli powder	⅛ oz/½ tsp

Method

1. Remove the head from the prawns, slit, devein and pat dry.

2. Mix malt vinegar, salt, red chilli powder, ginger and garlic pastes and marinate prawns in it for half an hour.

3. Place each prawn on a separate 10 inch square piece of greased aluminium foil.

4. Boil, drain and crush peas with a rolling pin.

5. Mix in cheese, onion, coriander, ginger, cumin, lemon juice, white pepper powder, tomato ketchup and pomegranate seeds.

6. Top each prawn with this mixture.

7. Grate cheese on each and wrap up the foil.

8. Place the parcels in a baking tray and bake in a preheated oven at 275 °F for 10-12 minutes.

Tips

Time
Preparation: 45 minutes
Cooking: 15 minutes

To Serve
Serve hot as a heavy snack

MEEN MOILY

*Small, fresh, sea fish in a thick brown curry with a liberal sprinkling
of whole red chillies popular in South India.*

Ingredients

Sole or plaice		Mustard (*sarson*) seeds	¼ oz/1 tsp
or small whole fresh fish	2 lb	Oil to fry fish	
Cardamoms	2	Onions, sliced	2½ oz/⅓ cup
Cinnamon	1" stick	Red chillies, whole	6
Cloves	2	Salt to taste	
Coconut, grated	4 oz/½ cup	Tamarind (*imlee*),	
Coriander, chopped	¼ oz/1 tsp	soaked in ½ cup water	¾ oz/4 tsp
Fenugreek (*methi*) seeds	⅛ oz/½ tsp	Tomatoes, chopped	4 oz/½ cup
Groundnut/peanut oil	2½ fl oz/⅓ cup	Turmeric (*haldi*) powder	¼ oz/1 tsp
Lemon juice	1 fl oz/2 tbs		

Method

1. Apply lemon juice to fish and leave for half an hour. Then wash with fresh water, squeeze lightly and pat dry. Fry the fish lightly in oil and set aside.

2. In a small pot heat 1 tablespoon/½ fl oz groundnut/peanut oil. Add mustard seeds, fenugreek seeds, cardamoms, cinnamon, cloves, whole red chillies and sauté lightly then cool. Blend to a smooth paste in a blender with the grated coconut.

3. Mash the soaked tamarind with your fingers, then squeeze out and discard the pulp. Keep the extract aside.

4. Heat the rest of the groundnut/peanut oil in a pot and sauté onions till brown. Add the tomatoes and turmeric and stir-cook for 4 to 5 minutes. Add the tamarind extract and bring to boil, reduce flame and let simmer for another 5 minutes.

5. Add coconut paste to the gravy. Cook till gravy thickens. Add salt and curry leaves.

6. Gently add the fried fish to the curry and simmer for 5 minutes.

Tips

Time
Preparation: 30 minutes
Cooking: 30 minutes

To Serve
Garnish with fresh coriander leaves and serve hot with boiled rice or roti

SERVES: 4

MACHHI TAMATAR

Cooked in thick tomato purée, the fish literally melts in the mouth.

Ingredients

Sole fish fillets	1-1¼ lb	Garlic, peeled and chopped	1 oz/6 tsp
Cashew nuts	¼ oz/1 tsp	Ginger paste	½ oz/1 tbs
Chilli powder	¼ oz/1 tsp	Oil	4 oz/½ cup
Coconut, grated	¼ oz/1 tsp	Lemon juice	1 oz/2 tbs
Coriander leaves, chopped	¼ oz/1 tsp	Salt to taste	
Cream	2½ fl oz/⅓ cup	Sunflower seeds	¼ oz/1 tsp
Garam masala	¼ oz/1 tsp	Tomatoes, chopped	10¾ oz/1¼ cups
Garlic paste	¼ oz/1 tsp		

Method

1. Marinate the fish in a mixture of the ginger and garlic pastes, salt, lemon juice and half the chilli powder. Set aside for half an hour.

2. Meanwhile, grind coconut, sunflower seeds and cashew nuts in a mixer.

3. Heat oil in a pot. Add fish and sauté lightly. Set aside.

4. In the remaining hot oil add the peeled garlic and sauté till golden brown. Add the tomatoes and stir-cook till the tomatoes are mashed.

5. Stir in the salt, left over red chilli powder and cook for 5 minutes.

6. Strain the gravy through a strainer and put on fire again. Add the coconut, sunflower seed and cashew nut paste, stir for 2-3 minutes.

7. Add the garam masala and the fried fish. Reserve 2 tablespoons cream for garnish and add the rest to the gravy. Let simmer for 2-3 minutes.

Time
Preparation: 45 minutes
Cooking: 30 minutes

To Serve
Garnish with fresh coriander leaves and cream. Serve hot with boiled rice

SAUCE NI MACHHI

A tangy, easy to make, light fish dish.

Ingredients

Shrimp/sole or plaice	1-1¼ lb	Vinegar	4 fl oz/½ cup
Chilli powder	⅛ oz/½ tsp		
Coriander leaves, chopped	1 oz/2 tbs	**For khichdi**	
Cumin (*jeera*) seeds	⅛ oz/½ tsp	Basmati rice	4 oz/½ cup
Eggs, whipped	2	Cumin (*jeera*) seeds	⅛ oz/½ tsp
Garlic, chopped	¼ oz/1 tsp	Clarified butter (*ghee*)	½ oz/1 tbs
Gram flour (*besan*)	1 oz/6 tsp	Fenugreek (*methi*) seeds	⅛ oz/½ tsp
Green chillies, chopped	4	Lentils	2 oz/¼ cup
Oil	1½ fl oz/3 tbs	Onions, sliced	2 oz/¼ cup
Sugar	1 oz/6 tsp	Turmeric (*haldi*) powder	¼ oz/1 tsp
Tomatoes, chopped	8¾ oz/1 cup		

Method

1. Apply salt to the fish and set aside for 10 minutes.

2. Heat the oil in a wok and fry garlic till pink.

3. Add cumin, coriander leaves, chillies and gram flour. Sauté together till light brown.

4. Add the chopped tomatoes, 16 fl oz/ 2 cups water and cook for 4 minutes. Season.

5. Add the fish and cook for 2-3 minutes. Remove from fire.

6. Beat the eggs with vinegar, then heat the mixture in another pan. Add to the fish and gravy. Return the kadhai to very low heat and cook for 6 minutes.

For khichdi

Wash rice and lentils in plenty of water, then soak for 15 minutes. Fry onions in the ghee till brown. Add turmeric, cumin and fenugreek and sauté. Drain rice and lentils and add to the pan. Fry for 3-4 minutes. Add 12 fl oz/1½ cups boiling water, cover and cook till rice and lentils are well mashed, about 10-15 minutes.

Time
Preparation: 30 minutes
Cooking: 30 minutes

To Serve
Serve fish with khichdi, pickles and poppadams

PRAWN BALCHAO

This is a favorite Goan dish which can be preserved for a couple of days.
In fact, its tangy taste is at its best after a day or so. It can be stored
as a pickle for longer, if preservatives are added.

Ingredients

Prawns, small size	2.2 lb		Ginger paste	1 oz/2 tbs
Black peppercorns	1/8 oz/1/2 tsp		Groundnut/peanut oil	5 fl oz/2/3 cup
Cardamoms	12		Malt vinegar	5 fl oz/2/3 cup
Cinnamon	4 sticks, 1" each		Onions, chopped	5 oz/2/3 cup
Cloves	1/4 oz/15		Red chillies, whole	15
Cumin (*jeera*) seeds	1/8 oz/1/2 tsp		Sugar	1 oz/6 tsp
Curry leaves	12		Tomatoes, chopped	4 oz/1/2 cup
Garlic paste	1 oz/2 tbs			

Method

1. Shell, devein, wash and pat dry prawns.

2. Blend the peppercorns, cardamoms, cinnamon, cloves, cumin and red chillies with the vinegar in a blender. Keep aside.

3. Heat oil in a wok and deep fry prawns to a golden brown. Remove.

4. Add the onions to the hot oil. Sauté till golden brown. Add the ginger and garlic pastes and stir for a minute.

5. Add the tomatoes and the blended paste.

6. Stir for 2-3 minutes.

7. Add the fried prawns, curry leaves and sugar and cook till prawns are tender.

Time	**To Serve**
Preparation: 30 minutes	Serve hot with steamed rice or any
Cooking: 30 minutes	Indian bread

SERVES: 4

KOLMINO PATIO

A hot, sweet and sour prawn delicacy popular with Parsis.

Ingredients

Prawns	2 lb	Lemon juice	¾ fl oz/4 tsp
Cinnamon	2 sticks, 1" each	Oil	2½ fl oz/⅓ cup
Cloves	5	Onions, chopped	5 oz/⅔ cup
Coriander leaves, chopped	½ oz/1 tbs	Red chilli powder	¼ oz/1 tsp
Coriander seeds	¼ oz/1 tsp	Red chillies, whole	5
Cumin (*jeera*) seeds	¼ oz/1 tsp	Salt to taste	
Garlic paste	¾ oz/4 tsp	Tamarind (*imlee*)	1½ oz/3 tbs
Jaggery/brown sugar	2½ oz/5 tbs	Turmeric (*haldi*) powder	¼ oz/1 tsp

Method

1. Shell, devein ,wash and pat dry the prawns.
2. Put whole red chillies, garlic paste, coriander seeds, cloves, cinnamon, turmeric, cumin seeds and red chilli powder in a blender and make a paste with approximately 2 fl oz/¼ cup water.
3. Soak tamarind in half cup water and extract juice.

4. Heat fat in a kadhai and sauté onions till golden brown. Add the paste and salt and stir till the fat surfaces.
5. Add prawns and stir for 2 to 3 minutes. Add 16 fl oz/2 cups water, bring to boil and simmer till the prawns are cooked.
6. Add the tamarind, jaggery/brown sugar and lemon juice and mix well.

Time	**To Serve**
Preparation: 45 minutes	Garnish with chopped coriander
Cooking: 25 minutes	leaves. Tastes best with brown rice

SERVES: 4

KID NU GOSHT

A combination of lamb and potatoes cooked in a spicy gravy.

Ingredients

Lamb	1 lb	Ginger paste	¼ oz/1 tsp
Bay leaf (*tej patta*)	1	Green chillies	4
Black peppercorns	⅛ oz/½ tsp	Onions, chopped	5 oz/⅔ cup
Cashew nuts	2½ oz/⅓ cup	Poppy seeds	⅛ oz/½ tsp
Cinnamon	2" stick	Potatoes, diced	6 oz/¾ cup
Cloves	4	Salt to taste	
Coconut milk	8 fl oz/1 cup		
Cooking oil	2½ fl oz/⅓ cup	**Note**	
Cumin (*jeera*) seeds	⅛ oz/½ tsp	Lamb shanks are ideal for this dish. However,	
Garlic paste	¼ oz/1 tsp	any stewing cuts or 2" pieces are suitable.	

Method

1. Marinate the lamb in half the ginger and garlic pastes for 2 hours.
2. In a non-stick pan heat the oil and sauté the onions till reddish brown. Add the remaining ginger and garlic pastes, cumin seeds, salt, poppy seeds, cashew nuts, green chillies and the whole spices (cinnamon, cloves and black peppercorns).

Sauté for 5 minutes on a moderate flame.
3. Add meat pieces and sauté for 8-10 minutes. Every few minutes sprinkle with a tablespoon of water to keep contents of the pan moist. Add 16 fl oz/2 cups water and potatoes. Cover and stew till meat is tender.
4. Add the coconut milk, simmer for a minute then remove from fire.

Time
Preparation: 2¼ hours
Cooking: 1½ hours

To Serve
Serve hot with steamed rice

RARA MEAT

Lamb pieces stir-cooked painstakingly in a spicy gravy.

Ingredients

Lamb cuts	2.2 lb	Ginger paste	1½ oz/3 tbs
Bay leaves (*tej patta*)	2	Oil	5 fl oz/²⁄₃ cup
Black cardamoms	3	Onions, chopped	8¾ oz/1 cup
Cardamoms	8	Red chilli powder	¼ oz/1 tsp
Coriander powder	1 oz/6 tsp	Red chillies, whole	4
Cumin (*jeera*) powder	¼ oz/1 tsp	Salt to taste	
Garlic, chopped	¾ oz/4 tsp	Tomatoes, chopped	5 oz/²⁄₃ cup
Garlic paste	1½ oz/3 tbs	Turmeric (*haldi*) powder	⅛ oz/½ tsp
Ginger, shredded	¾ oz/4 tsp	Yoghurt	5 oz/²⁄₃ cup

Method

1. Whip together the yoghurt and salt and marinate the lamb in it for an hour.

2. Heat the oil in a pot and crackle both the bay leaves and cardamoms in it.

3. Add the onions and sauté till light brown. Add ginger and garlic pastes and stir for 4 to 5 minutes. Stir in coriander, turmeric and red chilli powders.

4. Add the lamb with the marinade, bring to boil then reduce flame. Let simmer, adding 3 teaspoons water at intervals. Cook until tender.

5. Add the tomatoes, chopped garlic and ginger and stir. Then add the cumin and whole red chillies. Cook on low flame till the lamb pieces are coated with the masala and tender.

Time
Preparation: 1½ hours
Cooking: 1½ hours

To Serve
Serve with a tandoori bread of your choice

GOSHT KALIA

*Cardamom flavored lamb has silver leaf and saffron to set off the
creamy gravy beneath.*

Ingredients

Lamb curry cuts	2 lb	Onions, chopped	3 oz/6 tbs
Almond paste	1 oz/2 tbs	Saffron	a pinch
Cardamom powder	¼ oz/1 tsp	Salt to taste	
Fresh cream	1 fl oz/2 tbs	Silver leaf	
Garlic paste	¼ oz/1 tsp	Sweet ittar	a few drops
Ginger paste	¼ oz/1 tsp	White butter	2 oz/¼ cup
Green chillies, chopped	2	Yoghurt	2 oz/¼ cup

Method

1. Put lamb cuts in a pan of water and bring to boil. Drain and wash pieces.

2. Put the blanched lamb pieces, together with chopped onions, ginger and garlic pastes, yoghurt, butter, chillies, salt and half the cardamom powder in a pan and simmer.

Ensure that the meat does not wok unevenly. Cook till lamb is tender.

3. Add the almond paste and cook till the gravy thickens.

4. Finish off by adding the rest of the cardamom powder, sweet ittar and cream.

Time
Preparation: 30 minutes
Cooking: 1½ hours

To Serve
Remove to a serving dish, place silver leaf on top and sprinkle with saffron crushed in a teaspoonful of water. Serve with any Indian bread

Taar Korma

Boneless lamb cooked with dry spices and nuts.

Ingredients

Lamb, boneless, diced	2 lb	Garlic paste, browned	1 oz/2 tbs
Lamb stock	32 fl oz	Ginger paste	1 oz/2 tbs
Almonds	½ oz/1 tbs	Mace (*javitri*) powder	a pinch
Cardamoms	2	Oil	3 oz/6 tbs
Cardamom powder	a pinch	Onion paste, browned	1 oz/2 tbs
Cashew nuts	½ oz/1 tbs	Saffron	a pinch
Chilli powder	¼ oz/1 tsp	Salt to taste	
Cinnamon	1" stick	Sunflower seeds	½ oz/1 tbs
Cloves	4	Sweet ittar	few drops
Dough to seal dish		Tomato purée	4 fl oz/½ cup
Garlic paste	1 oz/2 tbs	Yoghurt	4 oz/½ cup

Method

1. Heat oil in a wok and crackle whole spices (cardamoms, cloves and cinnamon). Add ginger and garlic pastes. Sauté till almost dry.
2. Add the lamb pieces along with chilli powder, onion paste, yoghurt, tomato purée, salt and stock. Cook till the meat is half done. Add the browned garlic paste and continue cooking till the lamb is tender.
3. Remove lamb pieces to an oven proof dish. Strain the gravy into another pot.
4. Meanwhile, blanch almonds and deep fry till golden brown. Deep fry sunflower seeds and cashew nuts separately till golden brown. Mix the three in a blender with 4 tablespoons of water and make a brown colored nut paste. Add to the strained gravy and cook for 2 to 3 minutes.
5. Pour the gravy over the lamb pieces.
6. Sprinkle with mace and cardamom powders, saffron and sweet ittar. Cover and seal the dish with dough and cook in a preheated oven at 275 °F for 10 minutes.

Tips

Time
Preparation: 30 minutes
Cooking: 1½ hours

To Serve
Remove cover and wipe edges of the dish. Serve hot with boiled rice or roti

SERVES: 4

KARELI KA ROGAN JOSH

Lamb shins cooked in a smooth gravy and simmered in an oven till tender.

Ingredients

Lamb shins	2 lb/8 pieces	Ginger paste	1 oz/2 tbs
Almond paste	½ oz/1 tbs	Oil	¾ fl oz/4 tsp
Cardamoms	5	Onion paste, browned	1 oz/2 tbs
Chilli powder	¼ oz/1 tsp	Saffron	a pinch
Cloves	3	Salt to taste	
Coriander leaves, chopped	½ oz/1 tsp	Stock	24 fl oz/3 cups
Dough to seal dish		Sweet ittar	a few drops
Garam masala	⅛ oz/½ tsp	Tomato purée	4 fl oz/½ cup
Garlic paste	1 oz/2 tbs	Yoghurt	1½ oz/3 tbs
Ginger juliennes	¼ oz/1 tsp		

Method

1. Heat the oil, crackle the cloves and the cardamoms, add the ginger and garlic pastes and sauté till almost dry.

2. Add lamb shins, salt, yoghurt, browned onion paste and chilli powder. Stir for 3-5 minutes. Add stock and simmer till meat is tender.

3. Remove shins into an ovenproof casserole and strain the curry into another pan.

4. Add the tomato purée to the strained curry and cook till only two-thirds of the liquid is left.

5. Stir in the almond paste and the garam masala. Cook for 2-3 minutes. Pour over the cooled shins.

6. Sprinkle with ginger juliennes, chopped coriander, saffron (crushed in a few drops of water) and sweet ittar. Seal the casserole with dough and let simmer for 5 minutes in a preheated oven.

Tips

Time
Preparation: 30 minutes
Cooking: 2 hours

To Serve
Open the seal and wipe edges of dish. Serve hot with taftan. For recipe see p. 59 of the **Tandoor & Dry Dishes** section

43

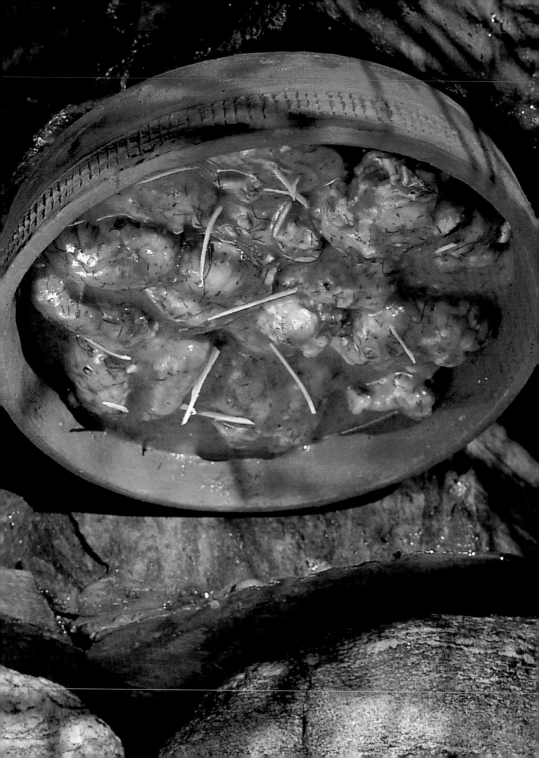

MAGAZ KALIA

Brain curry cooked with care to get a dark, thick, gravy.

Ingredients

Lamb brains	6, each 3 oz	Garam masala	$^1/_8$ oz/$^1/_2$ tsp
Black pepper powder	$^1/_8$ oz/$^1/_2$ tsp	Garlic paste	$^1/_4$ oz/1 tsp
Chilli powder	$^1/_4$ oz/1 tsp	Ginger juliennes	$^1/_4$ oz/1 tsp
Cooking oil	3 fl oz/6 tbs	Ginger paste	$^1/_4$ oz/1 tsp
Coriander leaves, chopped	$^1/_2$ oz/1 tbs	Lemon juice	2 fl oz/4 tbs
Coriander powder	$^1/_4$ oz/1 tsp	Onion paste	$3^1/_2$ oz/7 tbs
Fenugreek (*kasoori methi*)		Salt to taste	
leaves, dry, rubbed	$^1/_8$ oz/$^1/_2$ tsp	Turmeric (*haldi*) powder	$^1/_4$ oz/1 tsp
Fenugreek (*methi*) seeds	$^1/_8$ oz/$^1/_2$ tsp	Yoghurt	4 fl oz/$^1/_2$ cup

Method

1. Immerse the brains in water with half the turmeric, 3 tablespoons lemon juice and half of the ginger and garlic pastes and salt. Bring to boil. Simmer for 10 minutes then remove brains carefully.

2. Whip yoghurt with the remaining turmeric, ginger and garlic pastes, chilli powder and onion paste.

3. Heat oil in a wok and crackle the fenugreek seeds. Add coriander powder and the yoghurt mixture and stir-fry until oil surfaces.

4. Add the brains and half cup water. Cover and cook for 4-5 minutes.

5. Add garam masala, black pepper and fenugreek leaves. Cook on low heat for 2 minutes.

Time
Preparation: 20 minutes
Cooking: 30 minutes

To Serve
Serve garnished with chopped coriander, ginger juliennes and a sprinkling of lemon juice

ACHAARI GOSHT

A lamb delicacy with a pickled effect which tastes best when fresh.

Ingredients

Leg of lamb	2.2 lb	Mustard oil (*sarson ka tel*)	¾ fl oz/4 tsp
Asafoetida (*heeng*)	a pinch	Mustard (*sarson*) seeds	⅛ oz/½ tsp
Cloves	5	Onion seeds (*kalonji*)	⅛ oz/½ tsp
Cooking oil	2 fl oz /4 tbs	Red chilli powder	¼ oz/1 tsp
Cumin (*jeera*) seeds	¼ oz/1 tsp	Red chillies, whole	6
Garlic, shredded	¼ oz/1 tsp	Salt to taste	
Ginger, shredded	¼ oz/1 tsp	Turmeric (*haldi*) powder	⅛ oz/½ tsp
Jaggery/brown sugar	1 oz/6 tsp	Yoghurt	8¾ oz/1 cup
Lemon juice	1 fl oz/2 tbs		

Method

1. Clean and cut lamb into 1 inch pieces. Put to boil with 5 cups of water, turmeric and salt. Reduce heat and simmer till lamb is tender. Remove pieces and reserve stock.

2. Smoke mustard oil in a pan, reduce flame and add the other cooking oil. Add whole red chillies and sauté till chillies turn black, then discard the chillies.

3. Crackle mustard seeds, cloves and asafoetida in the oil.

4. Add the lamb pieces, red chilli powder, cumin seeds, onion seeds, jaggery/brown sugar, ginger and garlic and stir. Cook till the meat pieces turn brown.

5. Stir in stock and lemon juice and simmer for 2 minutes. Reduce flame and stir in the yoghurt stirring vigorously. Cook till the fat surfaces.

Time
Preparation: 30 minutes
Cooking: 1 hour

To Serve
Serve with naan or paratha. Garnish with deep fried onion rings, if desired

HANDI PASINDA

An aromatic lamb dish laced with the flavor of crackled whole spices.

Ingredients

Lamb pieces (2" x 4")	1½ lb	Coriander leaves, chopped	¼ oz/1 tsp
Bay leaf (*tej patta*)	1	Garam masala	¼ oz/1 tsp
Black cardamoms	2	Garlic cloves	1½ oz/3 tbs
Black pepper powder	⅛ oz/½ tsp	Ginger	1 oz/1 sq" piece
Cardamom powder	⅛ oz/½ tsp	Onions, sliced	8¾ oz/1 cup
Cinnamon	1" stick	Poppy seeds	½ oz/1 tbs
Cloves	6	Red chilli powder	¼ oz/1 tsp
Cooking oil	4 fl oz/½ cup	Yoghurt	8¾ oz/1 cup

Method

1. Heat oil in a wok and sauté half the onions till golden brown. Remove.

2. Peel and chop the ginger and the garlic. Mix with the browned and raw onions and poppy seeds and blend to a fine paste with 1 fl oz/2 tablespoons water.

3. Heat the oil left in the wok and crackle the black cardamoms, cinnamon, bay leaf and cloves. Add blended paste and sauté for 3 to 4 minutes.

4. Add yoghurt and cook for 4 to 5 minutes. Add the lamb pieces and cook for another 3-4 minutes till the fat surfaces.

5. Transfer to a casserole. Add 4 fl oz/½ cup water. Sprinkle red chilli powder, garam masala, cardamom powder and black pepper powder on top. Cover and cook in a preheated oven at 275 °F for 10 minutes.

Time
Preparation: 30 minutes
Cooking: 45 minutes

To Serve
Garnish with coriander, wipe the edges of the dish and serve with naan

SAFED KEEMA

The uniqueness of this preparation lies in the fact that red meat turns into a white gravy dish.

Ingredients

Lamb ground	1½ lb	Green chillies, whole	4
Almonds	½ oz/1 tbs	Onions, chopped	2½ oz/⅓ cup
Cardamom powder	⅛ oz/½ tsp	Poppy seeds (*khus khus*)	½ oz/3 tsp
Cashew nuts	½ oz/1 tbs	White pepper powder	¼ oz/1 tsp
Cooking oil	2 fl oz/4 tbs	Yoghurt	8¾ oz/1 cup
Garlic, chopped	½ oz/1 tbs		

Method

1. Soak and peel almonds. Soak cashew nuts and poppy seeds for an hour and blend all three with a little water to a fine paste.

2. Heat oil in a wok and sauté onions and garlic on low flame without letting them turn brown.

3. Add minced meat and sauté over gentle heat.

4. Whip and add the yoghurt, cardamom powder, white pepper powder and whole green chillies.

5. Simmer gently till minced meat is cooked and gravy is reduced by half.

6. Pick out and discard the green chillies.

7. Add the nut paste and stir well. Simmer for 2-3 minutes.

Time
Preparation: 30 minutes
Cooking: 45 minutes

To Serve
Serve hot with paratha. For recipe see p. 61 of the ***Tandoor & Dry Dishes*** section

GOSHT KOFTA

Spicy mince meat balls in a thick brown gravy, redolent with whole spices.

Ingredients

Ground meat	1¼ lb	Green chillies, chopped fine	6
Cardamoms	4	Melon seeds (*magaz*)	¼ oz/½ tbs
Cinnamon	1" stick	Oil	3 fl oz/6 tbs
Cinnamon powder	⅛ oz/½ tsp	Onions, chopped fine	8¾ oz/1 cup
Cloves	6	Onion paste	4 oz/½ cup
Coconut, grated	¼ oz/½ tbs	Onion paste, browned	¼ oz/1 tsp
Coriander leaves, chopped	¼ oz/1 tsp	Poppy seeds (*khus khus*)	¼ oz/1 tsp
Coriander powder	½ oz/1 tbs	Red chilli powder	¼ oz/1 tsp
Egg white	1	Salt to taste	
Garlic paste	¼ oz/1 tsp	Turmeric (*haldi*) powder	⅛ oz/½ tsp
Ginger, chopped fine	½ piece	Yoghurt	8¾ oz/1 cup
Ginger paste	½ oz/3 tsp		

Method

1. Mix egg white, salt, red chilli powder, cinnamon powder, half the ginger and garlic pastes and all of the browned onion paste with the ground meat.

2. Mix together chopped onions, green chillies, coriander and chopped ginger.

3. Form walnut sized balls of the Ground meat, stuffing a bit of the onion, chilli, coriander and ginger mix in the centre. Keep aside.

4. Make a blend of the grated coconut, poppy and melon seeds in a blender with 1 fl oz/2 tablespoons water.

5. Heat oil in a flat pan and crackle cloves, cinnamon and cardamoms. Add turmeric, coriander powder, the remaining ginger and garlic pastes, onion paste and the blended seed paste. Stir-cook till the fat surfaces. Add whiped yoghurt. Cook for 5 minutes.

6. Add 16 fl oz/2 cups water and bring to boil. Gently slide in the meat balls (koftas), a few at a time, keeping the gravy boiling. When all the koftas are in, reduce heat and simmer.

7. Turn koftas over and cook till firm and tender. Let gravy thicken.

Time
Preparation: 30 minutes
Cooking: 30 minutes

To Serve
Garnish with coriander leaves and serve with any Indian bread

SERVES: 4

NARGISI KOFTA

'Doe eyed' eggs covered with mince, floating in a clean curry.

Ingredients

Lean lamb, finely ground	1 lb	Mace (*javitri*) powder	a pinch
Cardamom powder	⅛ oz/½ tsp	Oil to deep fry	
Cashew nuts	1 oz/2 tbs	Onions, chopped	4 oz/½ cup
Cooking oil	3 fl oz/6 tbs	Poppy seed (*khus khus*) paste	½ oz/1 tbs
Coriander powder	¼ oz/1 tsp	Red chilli powder	¼ oz/1 tsp
Coriander leaves, chopped	⅛ oz/½ tsp	Roasted gram daal,	
Garlic paste	¾ oz/4 tsp	powdered	1¼ oz/3 tbs
Ginger paste	½ oz/3 tsp	Salt to taste	
Ginger juliennes	⅛ oz/½ tsp	Yoghurt	4 oz/½ cup
Hard boiled eggs	4		

Method

1. Mix salt, gram daal powder, poppy seed paste, half the red chilli powder and quarter of ginger paste with the mince. Peel and wash eggs.

2. Divide the minced meat mixture into four. Wrap each portion evenly around an egg, first moistering your hands with a little water, to seal all sides.

3. Refrigerate till firm. Deep fry over moderate heat.

4. Cut each of the 4 pieces into halves. These will look like doe's eyes—hence the term 'nargisi' which means doe-eyed.

5. Heat the oil in a kadhai, brown half the onions and remove.

6. Grind together the remaining onions, cashew nuts, poppy seed paste and the browned onion.

7. Add rest of the ginger and garlic pastes to the left over oil. Cook till moisture evaporates.

8. Add coriander powder, red chilli powder and yoghurt and cook till the liquid is reduced to half.

9. Add the ground paste. Stir for 4 to 5 minutes. Add 12 fl oz/1½ cups water.

10. Simmer for 4 to 5 minutes and strain into another container. Add cardamom and mace powders. Arrange eggs in a dish and pour gravy over the eggs.

Tips

Time
Preparation: 30 minutes
Cooking: 45 minutes

To Serve
Garnish with ginger juliennes and coriander leaves. Serve hot with pulao or any Indian bread

SERVES: 4

RAAN-E-DUMPUKHT

An entire leg of lamb cooked to a melting smoothness with an assortment of spices,
prepared in the dumpukht or sealed pot style.

Ingredients

Leg of lamb	2.2 lb	Ginger paste	¼ oz/1 tsp
Black cumin		Green chillies, chopped	¼ oz/1 tsp
(*shah jeera*) seeds	¼ oz/1 tsp	Lemon juice	½ fl oz/1 tbs
Chaat masala	¼ oz/1 tsp	Malt vinegar	2½ fl oz/5 tbs
Cheese, grated	2 oz/¼ cup	Mint, chopped	¼ oz/1 tsp
Cocktail onions, chopped	¾ oz/4-5	Onion rings	4 oz/½ cup
Coriander leaves	¼ oz/1 tsp	Pineapple, chopped	8¾ oz/1 cup
Garam masala	⅛ oz/½ tsp	Red chilli powder	¼ oz/1 tsp
Garlic, chopped	1 oz/2 tbs	Salt to taste	
Garlic paste	¼ oz/1 tsp	White butter	2½ oz/5 tbs
Ginger, chopped	5 oz/⅔ cup		

Method

1. Remove the thigh bone from the leg of lamb. Marinate the meat in a mixture of red chilli powder, salt, ginger and garlic pastes and half the malt vinegar. Keep aside for hours.

2. Mix cocktail onions, ginger, green chillies, coriander, mint and garlic. Add the grated cheese and black cumin. Stuff the leg of lamb with this mixture.

3. Sew the open end of the leg with a needle and thread. Prick the leg with a fork.

4. Arrange the leg in a big baking tray. Pour over the remaining malt vinegar and sprinkle garam masala over it.

5. Cover with aluminium foil. Roast in a preheated oven for 1½ hours at 350 °F.

6. Heat butter in a pan. Sauté onion rings. Add chopped pineapple and garam masala. Mix well. Remove.

Tips

Time
Preparation: 2½ hours
Cooking: 2 hours

To Serve
Slice the leg open and garnish with pineapple and onion mixture. Squeeze lemon juice on top

HARA KEEMA

A mince delicacy garnished with a paste of fresh, green, leafy vegetables.

Ingredients

Lamb mince, coarsely ground	1½ lb	Green chillies, chopped	3
Cardamoms	2	Mint	½ oz/1 tbs
Cinnamon	1" stick	Oil	2 fl oz/4 tbs
Cloves	4	Onions, chopped	3oz/6 tbs
Coriander leaves	½ oz/1 tbs	Salt to taste	
Garam masala	⅛ oz/½ tsp	Spinach, boiled	2 oz/¼ cup
Garlic paste	½ oz/1 tbs	White pepper powder	⅛ oz/½ tsp
Ginger paste	½ oz/1 tbs	Yoghurt	8¾ oz/1 cup

Method

1. Make a paste of the spinach, mint and coriander leaves in a blender.

2. Heat oil in a kadhai. Crackle cloves, cardamom and cinnamon, add the ginger and garlic pastes and stir till the moisture evaporates.

3. Add the chopped onions and green chillies.

4. Stir in the mince, salt and white pepper. Stir-cook till the moisture evaporates.

5. Add yoghurt and cook till the liquid is reduced by half. Add the green leaves paste.

6. Cover and cook till mince is done. Add garam masala.

Tips

Time
Preparation: 20 minutes
Cooking: 40 minutes

To Serve
Goes best with khameeri roti. For recipe see p. 58 of the ***Tandoor & Dry Dishes*** section

LAMB BIRYANI

A Mughlai rice and meat dish. A meal in itself,
it can be served with only yoghurt as an accompaniment.

Ingredients

Lamb	2.2 lb/cut in 1" cubes	Ginger juliennes	¼ oz/1 tsp
Basmati rice	1.1 lb/2 cups	Mace (*javitri*) powder	a pinch
Butter, melted	1½ oz/3 tbs	Mint leaves, chopped	¼ oz/1 tsp
Cardamoms	5	Onions, chopped	4 oz/½ cup
Cinnamon	1" stick	Saffron	a pinch
Cloves	2	Salt to taste	
Cooking oil	3½ fl oz/7 tbs	Stock	16 fl oz/2 cups
Cream	4 fl oz/½ cup	Vetiver (*kewda*)	a few drops
Dough to seal dish		Red chilli powder	¼ oz/1 tsp
Ginger, chopped	1 oz/2 tbs	Yoghurt	4 oz/½ cup

Method

1. Heat oil in a pan and sauté chopped onions. Crackle cardamoms, cloves and cinnamon in the oil then add lamb pieces and sauté.

2. Add yoghurt, red chilli powder and salt. Stir till dry. Add stock and cook till meat is almost done.

3. In a separate pan boil rice in plenty of water, till the grains lengthen but are not fully cooked. Drain off the water.

4. Remove meat pieces from curry and spread in a heat-proof casserole. Strain curry. Reserve half and pour the remainder onto the meat. Sprinkle mace, mint, chopped ginger, vetiver and half the cream over the meat.

5. Place half the rice on the meat pieces. Sprinkle the reserved cream, the reserved liquid, melted butter and saffron, crushed in a spoonful of water over it.

6. Place rest of the rice on top. Cover and seal lid with dough. Cook over gentle heat for about 10-15 minutes.

Tips

Time
Preparation: 30 minutes
Cooking: 1½ hours

To Serve
Serve with bhuraani raita. For recipe see p. 62 of the **Vegetarian & Desserts** section

SERVES: 4

SORPOTEL

*This traditional, Goan pork and pork liver dish is a hot delicacy,
both literally and figuratively.*

Ingredients

Leg of pork	1½ lb	Ginger paste	3 oz/6 tsp
Pork blood	4 fl oz/½ cup	Groundnut/peanut oil	2 fl oz/4 tbs
Pork liver and heart	9 oz	Onions, sliced	5 oz/²⁄₃ cup
Black peppercorns	¼ oz/1 tsp	Red chillies, whole	15 nos
Butter	3 oz/6 tsp	Salt to taste	
Cardamom	4	Tomatoes, chopped	5 oz/²⁄₃ cup
Cloves	4	Turmeric (*haldi*) powder	¼ oz/1 tsp
Cumin (*jeera*) seeds	⅛ oz/½ tsp	Vinegar	½ fl oz/1 tbs
Garlic paste	¼ oz/1 tsp		

Method

1. Cut pork and liver into 1 inch cubes. Blanch liver by putting it in hot water with 2 teaspoons of salt and turmeric powder. Remove the pieces after a minute.

2. Heat oil in a pan and shallow fry the pork and liver pieces, separately, till golden brown. Remove and keep aside.

3. Mix vinegar with a tablespoon of water in a pan and bring to boil. Add the pork blood and boil till it is thick, about 8-10 minutes. Cool and freeze.

4. Put the garlic and ginger pastes, whole red chillies, peppercorns, cumin seeds, cloves and cardamoms with 2 tablespoons water in a blender and grind to a paste.

5. Heat the left-over oil again and sauté onions till golden brown. Add tomatoes and stir for a minute. Add the blended paste and cook till the fat surfaces. Add the pork with 5 cups water. Simmer till the pork is nearly cooked. Add the liver pieces and cook for 10 minutes.

6. Crush the frozen blood and stir it in. Add butter. Adjust seasoning.

Tips

Time
Preparation: 45 minutes
Cooking: 1¼ hours

To Serve
Remove to a deep bowl and serve with boiled rice

63

VINDALOO

*Another well known, hot, Goan delicacy. Vindaloo tastes better
when it is a day old and gets a pickled effect.*

Ingredients

Pork	1½ lb	
Black peppercorns	¼ oz/1 tsp	
Cardamoms	5	
Cinnamon	10 sticks of 1" each	
Cloves	5	
Coriander leaves, chopped	½ oz/1 tbs	
Cumin (*jeera*) seeds	⅛ oz/½ tsp	
Garlic paste	½ oz/1 tbs	
Ginger paste	1 oz/2 tbs	

Green chillies, chopped fine	4	
Groundnut/peanut oil	2½ fl oz/⅓ cup	
Malt vinegar	8 fl oz/1 cup	
Onions, chopped	2½ oz/⅓ cup	
Pickled onions (optional)	2½ oz/⅓ cup	
Potatoes, diced	14 oz/1⅔ cup	
Red chillies, whole	10	
Salt to taste		
Sugar	¼ oz/1 tsp	

Method

1. Cut the pork into 1 inch cubes. Pound the peppercorns, mix with half cup malt vinegar, sugar, cardamoms, green chillies and cloves and layer the pork pieces with this marinade overnight.

2. Make a paste of the whole red chillies, cinnamon, cumin seeds, turmeric, ginger and garlic pastes and the remaining vinegar with 2 fl oz/¼ cup water.

3. Heat oil in a pan. Deep fry potatoes till brown. Remove.

4. In the same hot oil sauté the onions till golden brown.

5. Add the paste and stir-cook till the fat surfaces.

6. Add the pork along with the marinade and stir for 3-4 minutes. Add 32 fl oz/4 cups water, bring to boil, reduce flame and simmer until pork is tender.

7. Add potatoes and pickled onions, if using them, and cook till potatoes soften.

Time

Preparation: 45 minutes plus overnight
for marination
Cooking: 1¼ hours

To Serve

Garnish with coriander leaves and
serve with boiled rice